A Practical Guide to Mentoring

Practical books that inspire

Learning to Counsel

How to develop the skills to work effectively with others

Feeling Good

Proven tools for lifelong happiness

Making the Most of Your Relationships

How to find satisfaction and intimacy with family and friends

Trusting Your Intuition

Harness the wisdom and power of your inner voice

A Practical Guide to Mentoring

Play an active and worthwhile part in the development of others, and improve your own skills in the process

DAVID KAY
and
ROGER HINDS

howtobooks

How To Books Ltd,
3 Newtec Place,
Magdalen Road,
Oxford, OX4 1RE, United Kingdom.
Tel: (01865) 793806. Fax: (01865) 248780.
email: info@howtobooks.co.uk
http://www.howtobooks.co.uk

British Library Cataloguing in Publication Data
A catalogue record for this book is available from the British Library.

Produced for How To Books by Deer Park Productions
Typeset by Anneset, Weston-super-Mare, North Somerset
Printed and bound by Cromwell Press, Trowbridge, Wiltshire

Contents

Preface

Mentoring is about one person helping another to achieve something. More specifically, it is about one person helping another to achieve something that is very important to them. It is about giving help and support in a non-threatening way, in a manner that the recipient will appreciate and value and that will empower them to move forward with confidence towards what they want to achieve. Mentoring is also concerned with creating an informal environment in which one person can feel encouraged to discuss their needs and circumstances openly and in confidence with another person who is in a position to be of positive help to them.

The need or even the necessity to achieve is present in all stages of life. At school and higher education there are standards to attain and examinations to be passed. If we have a hobby or a spare time interest, it is likely that we will be keen to get to grips with it as quickly as possible. When we start work we need to know the ins and outs of our job and what we are expected to do. In time, we may wish to consider the career prospects that exist in our current job and what we might aspire to. On a personal level, we may have set goals for achievement in the medium and long term. Clearly, we need help, advice and support in many aspects of life.

There are many sources of help that are linked to the attainment of goals. The formal structures within education, for instance, are designed to help students to complete their studies successfully. In the world of work, most organisations have systems of training and in-service development. Frequently, these are linked, and rightly so, to formal strategies for training and development, supported by processes of appraisal and performance review. Many of these approaches, have a common element – they take place in-house within the line management structure. Formal training and development structures are intended to be supportive and helpful. It is a fact of life, however, that some people do find it difficult, and possibly embarrassing, to discuss matters of a personal nature and their true career development intentions with those with whom they are in a line management relationship. In such cases, some other type of help and support is desirable.

Mentoring is an approach to people development that introduces an independent and objective source of help that is outside and independent of the line management relationship. It is being introduced, increasingly, into many different organisations and circumstances. Common examples are found during formal periods of training, in preparation for vocational or professional qualifications, in the introduction of new employees to new jobs and, at the opposite end of the structure, to help senior members of staff to prepare for their next posts. Mentoring also features within the academic sector – in the staff development processes of some colleges of further and higher education – and is also being used in schools to foster the development of gifted schoolchildren.

Whatever the circumstances, mentoring is an exclusive one-to-one relationship, is completely confidential and can be a useful complement to other staff development tools. This book explains what mentoring is . . . and what it is not! It takes you stage by stage through the process and shows how it can be of benefit to and an opportunity for development, both for the person being mentored and for the mentor.

David Kay and Roger Hinds

1

Helping People to Make Progress

Your role as a mentor will be to help your mentee to make decisions to enhance their progress towards specific goals. Mentoring is about helping people to make their own choices by suggesting options to them. It is not about telling them what to do or how to do it. Mentoring is a developing relationship encompassing a wide range of issues, not just those concerned with problem-solving – career, personal or family matters may arise. As your relationship with your mentee develops over time, such matters might gradually become part of their discussions with you as their mentor. Therefore, as you begin to consider your likely role, it is important to think about the broader aspects of people development and the factors that influence them in their daily work and their choice of career options.

In this chapter:

- understanding people's needs and expectations
- making career choices
- making progress
- sources of help
- advantages of 'off-line' help
- the mentoring approach.

It can be argued quite easily that people in working life today need help in their personal and career development. Life has become very complex, and the issues surrounding personal and career development are no less so. Within many trades and professions things are changing rapidly and there are more routes to the top than ever before. There are also many choices to be made at different stages of life, ranging from what to do after leaving school through to decisions later on that will affect family and career.

Because people vary so much as personalities and in their ambitions and career choices, it is important that whatever help they need is tailor-made to meet their particular needs and aspirations. It is also important that the help they get is objective, is given in an uncomplicated way and comes from a trusted and reliable source.

Self-assessment

- Have you knowledge and experience in a particular field?
- Do you keep up to date and are you able to take an objective view of the needs of others?
- Are you willing to use your knowledge and experience for their benefit?
- Do you have the enthusiasm to work with them independently and confidentially in helping them to plot their career path?

UNDERSTANDING PEOPLE'S NEEDS AND EXPECTATIONS

As a mentor, it is important to appreciate that each one of us has one thing in common: we are all individuals and we are living – acting and interacting with others – in the present and moving along the path of life. Most of us will have an aim in life and, in all probability, will have set an objective for ourselves; we might even have planned our life in stages. Thus, many of our actions will be geared towards achieving those objectives – in other words, helping us towards what we perceive to be our 'vision of the future'. To put it simply, if a possible course of action will move us towards our 'vision of the future', we will pursue it. If it won't, we will try something else.

The 'vision of the future' for each one of us will be different. It will depend upon our outlook on life, our aims and ambitions and on our particular circumstances:

- Whether we are single, married or in a relationship.
- Whether we have a family or other dependants.
- How we view work, particularly whether we see it as an opportunity for development and progression or just simply as a means of making a living and getting along.
- Where we (and our family, if we have one) want to be in the future, in terms of professional achievement and/or geographical location.
- The status we wish to have in society.

The 'vision of the future', quite simply, is whatever we want to achieve for ourselves (and our families) over the years ahead. This can be in terms of job, money, profession, status, where we wish to live, the type of house we want and things like that. In a 'family' situation, where both partners are working, this may entail discussion of 'whose job will determine where we live' and 'where are the best schools for our children'.

> *Most of us have a 'vision of the future' – what we want to achieve in life.*

MAKING CAREER CHOICES

For some people, work is regarded as the means of providing an existence for them and their dependants. However, for many, it is also the means of starting and progressing a career and the route by which the fulfilment of their ambition – their 'vision of the future' – is achieved.

In some cases, the idea of a possible career will have been nurtured from an early age. This might be because of academic excellence, because an area of work has been of particular interest at school or it may follow a family tradition. In other cases, the choice of career or line of work can be quite haphazard and be governed by the results of examinations (which might not be as expected) and the availability of jobs or study courses at a particular time.

Whatever our circumstances, deciding what to do after leaving school can be an anxious time. If we decide to go straight into a job we will need to consider 'which job?', 'will I be able to do it?' and, possibly, 'where will it lead?'. On the other hand, if we decide either to stay in education and undertake further study or to go straight into a training scheme where formal study will lead to a professional or vocational qualification, the questions to be asked are no less important. Whichever route we decide to take, we may need a great deal of help, advice and support, and that poses a crucial question: **Where can that help be found?**

> *Starting a new job or embarking on a career involves making choices. These choices can be facilitated by external help.*

MAKING PROGRESS

Initial training

As a mentor, it is important to recognise that there are several stages in life that can be difficult experiences and when help is needed. These may be when developing a new interest or starting a new job, whether that be straight from school, following a period of higher education or training, or from a previous employment. Whatever the circumstances, at the start, the new environment will seem to be strange. This will contrast with the 'cosiness' of the family environment, the 'protectiveness' of an academic or training institution or the familiarity within previous employment.

Starting formal study or a new job can be a traumatic experience.

New routines and new skills may have to be learned. Initial training will be necessary and professional knowledge, expertise and previous experiences will have to be incorporated into the procedures and systems of the new employer. It will also be necessary to work with new colleagues and to begin to operate with them as part of a team.

Initial training is important, but is only the first stage.

Embarking on a new interest or starting a new job entails going through a number of stages:

- Settling into new surroundings, getting acquainted with new people and acclimatising to the culture of the organisation, the environment and ways of working.
- Learning a new job that might involve routines that are unfamiliar.
- Achieving the desired levels of competence, output and productivity.

Progressing further

After initial training and experience, it should be possible for the individual to judge the extent to which they are likely to meet their immediate aims and objectives. Furthermore, depending upon the amount of help they have received already and the level of interest that is being shown in them as a person, it might even be possible to make some preliminary assessment of the likely long-term potential that exists and the degree to which what they are doing at present might begin to help them towards their longer-term objectives and their 'vision of the future'.

Further progression beyond the present position depends upon getting more information and advice.

They will need to consider issues such as the following:

- Their 'vision of the future' in terms of gaining further practical experience and/or qualifications.
- The opportunities that exist or are likely to arise with their present employer.
- Development opportunities within other organisations.

Getting further help and guidance is not always easy.

Clearly, a great deal of objective, unbiased and independent help and support will be necessary. Yet, again, that poses a crucial question: **Where can that help be found?**

SOURCES OF HELP

As we have seen, the need to obtain help and guidance that is objective and unbiased can arise at different times in an individual's development. By the same criteria, it can also be necessary during periods of study and when undertaking training schemes. Finding help that will be tailor-made to an individual may not always be easy. The question thus arises: **Where can help be found that is professional, objective and independent?**

A source of help and advice that is objective and independent can usually be found within the organisational framework of academic institutions. However, this may not be the case in other organisations, especially in the workplace. There, the immediate responsibility for training and development usually rests with an individual's line manager. Although many line managers are very professional and may have an objective view of development, not all would be able to give the broad, independent and unbiased help needed, for a number of reasons:

- They may not work at a sufficiently high level within the organisation, and therefore
- they may not be aware of the broader strategies of the organisation and, thus, of the in-house development opportunities available.

- They may be hesitant to advise on career opportunities in other organisations because they don't want to lose a good member of staff, because of loyalty to their employer or simply because they might not know, and therefore
- they may be less than objective in their approach to career development.
- They may be too busy in their day-to-day work!

There are other types of issue upon which an individual might need help. These might be job-related or involve relationships with colleagues or the boss. Unrelated domestic or family problems affecting work or study might exist and affect a person's ability to get on with their work and to make the progress that is expected. It might be difficult to raise such matters with a line manager or, if it is not a work-related issue, with the person closest to them. **Therefore, some other source of objective and independent help, outside the line or direct relationship, might be helpful**.

> *On-line help can often be limited by a number of factors.*

ADVANTAGES OF 'OFF-LINE' HELP

In order to be comfortable with work, training and career development, an individual may feel they would benefit from help and support from a source that is outside and independent of the 'line manager' or immediate relationship.

The person providing that kind of help should:

- have an independent and objective view of development;
- be able to form a clearer view of the ability and potential of the individual than they have of themselves;
- be up to date in technical and professional matters and be familiar with the requirements and the potential of any training programme being undertaken;
- be aware of development and/or promotional opportunities both within the present organisation and elsewhere;
- be able to devote the time necessary to provide help and support;
- be able to encourage and empower the individual to get the best from their work or any development or study programme; and
- have a personality and approach that encourages confidence in them and a sense of security that all matters discussed with them will be kept confidential.

Support from outside the line relationship can bring many benefits.

THE MENTORING APPROACH

The functions outlined form, in general terms, the role of a mentor and the qualities expected in those who undertake the role. In recent years, many organisations in different countries have recognised the value and potential of providing this kind of independent help and support. Countless individuals, at all levels within these organisations and in many professions, have come to regard *mentoring* as a valuable and even essential tool for their professional and personal support and development. Further, it is not only in formal organisations and settings that mentoring has been found to be helpful. For example, it has been used to good effect in helping people to develop 'out-of-work' interests and pastimes. Other beneficial spin-offs can result from the use of mentoring: many people, in both formal and informal circumstances and who have benefited from the help of a mentor, have gone on themselves to seek the role of mentor and thereby to help others.

Some types of mentoring

As already stated, mentoring can be helpful throughout all stages of personal and professional development, from the earliest beginnings to the highest level. The following are some of the instances where mentors have been helpful:

- At school or during periods of higher education (*the education mentor*).
- At the beginning of a new job (*the induction mentor*).
- During further training and development (*the training mentor*).

- When working towards a qualification (*the professional qualification mentor or the vocational qualification mentor*).
- In facilitating general development (*the mainstream mentor*).
- At the levels of top management (*the board-level or executive mentor*).
- In the development of a profession or a hobby (*the expert mentor*).
- In dealing with changes in life circumstances (*the general mentor*).

Mentoring is used widely by many organisations. Its use is detailed in the following chapter.

IN SUMMARY . . .

- Most people have their 'vision of the future' – an idea of what they want to achieve in life.
- Pursuit of the 'vision of the future', which will include 'family' as well as personal and professional issues, will take them beyond their present circumstances and involve discussion and agreement within their family or relationship.
- Embarking upon a career involves making choices, some of which are difficult without external help.
- Starting formal study or a new job or interest can be a difficult experience.

- Initial training in a new job is important, but is only the first stage in career progression.
- Further progress depends on developing additional skills and new interests and getting more information, advice and support.
- Getting objective advice, help and support is not always easy.
- 'On-line' help can often be limited by a number of factors.
- Advice, help and support from outside the immediate or line relationship can be helpful.
- 'Off-line' help is the basis of mentoring.
- The mentoring approach is used by many organisations in many sectors.
- There are different types of mentoring, depending upon the circumstances in which the mentoring takes place.

2

Mentoring and Who Can Do It

You will need to understand the role of the mentor, the different types of mentoring that are possible and the qualities and skills necessary in order to be successful. For the mentoring relationship to succeed, it is important to pay some attention to the matching of mentors with mentees and to the qualities and skills a mentor will need in order to be successful in the role.

In this chapter:

- a definition of mentoring
- some basic rules
- what is meant by 'off-line' relationship
- types of mentoring
- what you need to be a mentor
- ensuring compatibility of mentor and mentee.

There are many definitions of mentoring, all equally relevant in their own way. You will not need to know all the definitions that exist, but first you will need to have a basic understanding of the role of the mentor. Most of the rules relating to mentoring are flexible and vary according to the circumstances in which the mentoring is being undertaken, but there are a few basic rules that are common to all mentoring situations. The most important is that mentoring normally takes place outside the line management relationship, or 'off-line', and it is important that you recognise this at the outset.

There are many different types of mentoring and your approach and style should be appropriate for the type and circumstances of mentoring with which you are involved. If you are mentoring within different circumstances at the same time, you will need to adapt your style as you move between them. Whatever type of mentoring you undertake, you will need certain qualities and skills in order to be successful. Some of these you will have already; others you will acquire over time as you become more experienced in the mentoring role.

The success of any mentoring relationship will be improved significantly if care is taken at the outset to match mentors with mentees. Among other things this will go a long way to ensuring that there is a degree of compatibility between them.

Self-assessment

- Do you feel that you can work well 'off-line' in a mentoring relationship for the benefit of a mentee?
- In working 'off-line', can you do so without confusing

it with your managerial or line management responsibilities?

- Do you understand the purpose of mentoring and that this and the role of the mentor can differ according to the circumstances and the type of mentoring being undertaken?
- Do you possess the necessary qualities and skills and, if not, do you think you will be able to acquire them with experience?
- Are you prepared to accept that there is a need for a matching process of mentor and mentee in order to ensure that they will compatible in their mentoring relationship?

A DEFINITION OF MENTORING

From our experience of mentoring – from research and from running a large number of mentoring skills workshops – we have been able to consider the essential elements of the mentoring process. This has led us to the following definition, which we think will apply to any type of mentoring situation. Mentoring is: **a relationship between two parties, who are not connected within a line management structure, in which one party (the mentor) guides the other (the mentee) through a period of change and towards an agreed objective.**

This definition really says all there is to say about the process of mentoring and the mentoring relationship.

SOME BASIC RULES

It would be misleading to suggest that there are hard and fast rules for mentoring, as much depends on the type of mentoring being undertaken, the relationship between the mentor and the mentee and what they want to achieve. However, there are some basic rules you should follow if you are to be successful as a mentor and if the mentee is to get the help they expect from the mentoring relationship. These rules apply whether you are mentoring a new employee within your organisation, a member of staff undertaking a formal programme of professional training, a senior colleague preparing for a top-level post or whatever other circumstances in which you might be asked to undertake the role of mentor.

1. You must be seen to be independent

You will only be able to create an easy atmosphere with the mentee if they can be certain you are really an *independent* source of help. This means you should not be their line manager or elsewhere in the line management structure. It is only by being independent that you will be in a position to offer objective advice and support.

Maintain your independence. You should not be part of the mentee's line management structure.

2. Agree the purpose of your relationship

It is essential that, right at the outset, you and the mentee agree the nature of the mentoring being undertaken and the purpose and extent of your mentoring relationship. In doing this you should discuss and agree the timescale within which the mentoring will take place, the frequency of the contact between you and when the relationship will end.

3. Agree the means of contact

At the time you agree the nature of your relationship and frequency of contact you should also agree how the contact is to be made between you. There are many means available nowadays, even via the Internet, but the most common forms are by telephone and through meetings. Because frequent contact will be essential, the arrangements should be discussed and agreed right at the start.

Means of contact should be agreed at the outset.

4. Always stick to what you have agreed

Remember that the mentee is the more important partner in the relationship and that your role is to help them. Always try to stick to the agreed arrangements to contact them and never change the plan without good reason. If that does become necessary, always agree revised arrangements with them immediately. It is very easy, at a busy time when you are under pressure, to alter your arrangements with a mentee. This should not be done lightly, but if it is necessary, always try to fix an alternative date in your respective diaries as soon as possible. It can give a very bad impression of the mentor and of the mentoring scheme if a mentee is left 'hanging in the air' between meetings.

> *The mentee is the more important partner in the relationship.*

5. Always maintain confidentiality

It is important that your mentee feels they can trust you. In the course of your discussions they may wish to disclose matters of a personal nature that have a bearing on their work. You should maintain confidentiality at all times and the mentee should be confident that you will do that.

> *Maintain confidentiality at all times.*

WHAT IS MEANT BY 'OFF-LINE' HELP

In the mentoring context, working 'off-line' means that the mentor works outside and independently of the management structure within which the mentee works. This brings an immediate and essential benefit to the mentoring relationship. By being outside any line relationship with the mentee you can operate objectively and independently. This would not be possible if you are in a line relationship with the mentee and have some degree of management autonomy over them.

The mentor works independently of the management structure within which the mentee works.

In practice, therefore, as mentor, you should not be the mentee's line manager or in a line management relationship with them. This does not mean you cannot work within the same department. This is possible provided you are not within the same management 'line' and in a position where the mentee has some degree of accountability, however indirect, to you.

TYPES OF MENTORING

There is a variety of situations in which mentoring is used. Some were outlined briefly in the previous chapter. In order to complete the picture and to set the scene, they are listed again here, with a brief explanation of each.

1. The education mentor

Mentoring is now used frequently in schools and in institutes of higher education. At the higher-education level, mentoring schemes exist to help student teachers in their final year of training and in their first year after qualifying. Some universities use mentoring schemes to help newly appointed lecturers to settle into their roles.

2. The induction mentor

Many organisations designate a well-experienced member of

staff to help new employees in the early stages of employment, until the new employee feels confident in their new environment.

3. The training mentor

A training mentor is an experienced person, who is available to help new employees and those with changed responsibilities as they acquire new skills and adapt to change. They are there to help the mentee to get the best out of training. It is important not to confuse this role with that of the departmental trainer or training instructor, whose job it is to teach the new skills and routines that have to be learned.

A training mentor may also help trainees undertaking a formal practical training programme to get the best out of their work.

4. The professional qualification or vocational qualification mentor

The *professional qualification mentor* is a role that may be required by a professional institute. Their function is to guide a student towards qualification. In contrast, the *vocational qualification mentor* is concerned with helping an individual to prepare for and acquire a National Vocational Qualification. Their role is to guide the individual through their training and the gathering and presentation of their portfolio of evidence of experience, by which they prove their competence at the required standard.

With the move by some professional institutes towards the development of competence-based training, it may be important to recognise that some elements of the role of the vocational qualification mentor may need to be undertaken by a professional qualification mentor. Also, in some instances, these roles may operate alongside those of the training mentor and the mainstream mentor (see below).

5. The mainstream mentor

This is very much a general mentoring role and, in those organisations with a broad mentoring policy, will be the most common. The role of the mainstream mentor is to assist and guide at various stages of career development, through whatever transitions occur or may be anticipated.

This type of mentoring is found in many organisations. The following are just a few examples:

- To help junior managers and supervisors who may not have received formal training.
- In large organisations and some government departments, to support staff who have transferred from the head office into branches.
- To support staff in the management of new projects and in facing major job challenges.

6. The board-level or executive mentor

There is no reason why mentoring should be confined to staff at the beginning of their careers or who are developing within a profession or an organisation. Directors at board level can benefit from the service of a mentor. This is not uncommon and, frequently, a senior individual (possibly from outside the organisation) will provide support to directors and executives on strategic matters, career development and other issues associated with change.

7. The expert mentor

The role of an expert mentor can arise in a variety of circumstances. A mentor might be useful in the case of an individual starting a new hobby or pastime where the advice and help of someone already proficient can be invaluable. In addition, some schools have found that a mentor can be helpful in encouraging gifted children to develop in situations where their family circumstances may not be conducive to the desired development of the child.

8. The general mentor

In any circumstance of life, when approaching an occasion of change (whatever that may be), we can often benefit from the advice and support of someone who has experienced the same type of change before us. Although not included in the usual lists of mentoring circumstances, this broadening of the nature of mentoring is valid and can be valuable in a wide variety of situations. In our experience, anyone who helps another person to develop or to cope with change is acting in a mentoring role, although they may not recognise they are doing so.

WHAT YOU NEED TO BE A MENTOR

Mentoring is not an exclusive profession. Anyone who has the experience, interest and motivation to help a colleague through a period of transition can be a mentor. There are no formal qualifications for the role.

Qualities

To be a mentor, however, certain qualities are essential. To be successful you must have enthusiasm, commitment, willingness, approachability, an ability to open doors and relevant experience. An ability to treat with the utmost confidentiality everything you are told and discuss within the mentoring relationship is also essential.

> *Enthusiasm and commitment are important. Confidentiality is essential.*

Knowledge

You must also make sure that you know or are prepared to get to know something about the mentee themselves. Naturally, the precise information you need will depend on the particular circumstances and the purpose of the mentoring you are undertaking. For example, if you are mentoring for a programme of professional or personal development, details of the mentee's objectives and programme of development will be essential. In some cases it is also useful to know something about the mentee's personal life and circumstances. This might apply if they are undertaking a programme of formal study and have to complete certain coursework or assignments in their own time and where their ability to do so might be affected by their home circumstances.

> *There will be a need to know the individual's programme of development.*

Experience and qualifications

In some cases it is useful if you have relevant experience. As indicated in the descriptions given earlier in this chapter, this might be particularly useful in the case of induction, mainstream or board-level mentoring.

> *Relevant experience is useful in certain circumstances but not all.*

This might not be so necessary for other types of mentoring, but in the case of an individual who is studying for a professional qualification, you must familiarise yourself with the syllabus and professional development requirements. It is not always necessary to hold the same qualification as that being studied for by the mentee. Although in certain circumstances this may have advantages, the personal qualities listed here are more relevant.

> *Relevant experience is useful in certain circumstances, but it is not always necessary to hold the same professional qualification as the mentee.*

Sometimes, a fresh look from a different perspective can be beneficial.

Personal skills

To be effective as a mentor you will need to apply a number of other personal skills. These will include:

- listening
- motivating
- influencing
- fact-finding
- liaising
- counselling
- time management
- staff development.

However, it is not necessary for you to have direct training or tutoring skills as these elements are more properly the function of the line manager or tutor rather than the mentor.

You do not necessarily have to possess all the necessary

personal skills at the start. In fact, the very process of being a mentor can enable you to develop them.

You need to be aware of the skills required.

ENSURING COMPATIBILITY OF MENTOR AND MENTEE

For mentoring to be successful there needs to be a degree of compatibility between yourself and the person who will be your mentee. If you are part of a mentoring scheme, there should be someone who acts as the mentoring scheme co-ordinator. Usually, they will be responsible for matching mentors with mentees. It will be their task to make sure there is a strategy in place for this. This strategy should include liaison with proposed mentors and mentees in order to ensure they are likely to be compatible in forming a good mentoring relationship.

The scheme co-ordinator is usually responsible for matching strategy.

There are two crucial factors that should be taken into account when matching mentors and mentees:

1. The mentor must want to take on the role.
2. The styles and personalities of the mentor and mentee must be compatible.

These factors can be determined by a simple questionnaire to ascertain what each party expects from the relationship and how they would view the mentoring process in practice.

Some other very important factors should be considered during the process of matching:

- *The mentor must be easily accessible to the mentee.* It should be relatively easy for a mentee to make contact with their mentor, by whatever means is agreed between them. If this is not going to be possible, the particular mentoring relationship should not be considered.
- *The mentor should not hold the purse strings.* This is crucial because the mentor is not going to be able to function independently and objectively if they have any responsibility for the budget from which the mentee's development would be financed; and, as covered earlier:
- *The mentor must* not *have any line relationship with the mentee.*

IN SUMMARY . . .

Mentoring is a process in which a mentor helps a mentee through a period of change. Successful mentoring requires that a few basic rules are followed:

- Both parties must agree the purpose and extent of their relationship:
  - the means and frequency of contact must be agreed;
  - they must stick to the agreement; and
  - absolute confidentiality must be maintained.

- The mentor should not be in a line management relationship to the mentee.
- Mentoring can be a useful means of development at all levels, from new entrants to board level.
- Mentoring is not an exclusive profession. The important qualities to be an effective mentor are enthusiasm, commitment, willingness and an ability to 'open doors'.
- Mentoring can be a means of development for the mentor as well as the mentee.
- A means of 'matching' mentor with mentee is essential in order to ensure compatibility between the two.

3

Preparing Yourself for the Role

You will need to spend some time in both preparing yourself to undertake the role of mentor and also for your initial contact with the mentee. It is important too, that the mentee understands the mentoring function and is properly prepared. You should play a part in this in order to ensure that the relationship gets off on a sound footing from the very start and that there are no misunderstandings.

In this chapter:

- understanding the mentoring process
- clarifying objectives
- obtaining background information
- the roles of other parties
- your role in preparing the mentee
- the first meeting.

Before agreeing to undertake the role of mentor it is important that you carry out some personal preparation. You will need to ensure that you fully understand the mentoring process and are able to distinguish it from other management and development processes such as tutoring, coaching, counselling and staff appraisal. You will need to ensure that you are clear in your own mind about the objectives of mentoring and in particular the purpose of the individual relationship that you are about to undertake.

In order to do this and to get the relationship off to a good start, you will need to make sure you have as much relevant background information as possible. This will include the purpose for which the mentoring is being undertaken (e.g. is it to help the individual to achieve a specific objective, such as becoming professionally qualified, or to assist in their career development?). Some knowledge of the individual's previous experience in the particular field and something about their personal background, hobbies and interests will also be useful.

You will also need to make yourself aware of the roles of other parties involved with your mentee. You will then need to ensure that you do not clash with the roles of others. A clear understanding of their role and relationship with the mentee at the outset will help to avoid this.

In any mentoring relationship the first meeting is important and often sets the tone for the future. It is vital, therefore, that you prepare for this and don't go into it without a proper plan as to how it should be structured.

Even if you do all these things, the purpose will not be achieved unless your mentee has also undertaken some personal preparation. Your part in helping them to prepare can be vital and it will make your task much easier when you come to carry out the mentoring role.

Self-assessment

- Have you the discipline to plan and prepare or are you the sort of person who prefers to act on instinct?
- If you do plan and prepare, are you happy to be flexible with your plans if circumstances indicate the need to change them?
- Are you able to distinguish between the mentoring role and other staff development tools?
- Do you think you would be able to help someone to prepare for the mentee role without influencing them unduly towards your way of doing things?

UNDERSTANDING THE MENTORING PROCESS

Before undertaking the mentoring role it is essential you understand the process and the difference between mentoring and other personal development roles. Being an off-line relationship, mentoring must not be confused with coaching, tutoring, appraisal or counselling (although a counselling-style approach may be adopted). Neither should it include any form of disciplinary process. It is also a confidential relationship between mentor and mentee and this confidence must be respected at all times.

The process may differ in approach according to the type of mentoring being undertaken, and you must give thought to this before your first meeting with your mentee:

You must make sure you understand the process and the difference with other forms of personal development.

- Make sure you fully understand the process and the relationship before you start.
- Don't confuse it with other personal development tools.
- Ensure that you fully appreciate the possible time commitment.
- Ensure that you fully understand the mentor's role.
- Consider the range of issues that might be raised and the demands that might be placed upon you.
- Remember that mentoring is about helping another individual to achieve their objectives and not about imposing your own aims and objectives on them.

To be a successful mentor you must understand the role and the process.

CLARIFYING OBJECTIVES

Each mentoring scheme and sometimes each relationship within a scheme will have different objectives, and it is important that you clarify these at the outset and before you begin the process.

Generally speaking, the objective of a mentoring scheme is to assist another individual (the mentee) to achieve a particular goal. The emphasis must be on *helping* them through a process and not doing the work for them or dictating to them how it must be done. You must therefore be prepared to find out what help they need from the relationship and then plan to act accordingly.

You should bear in mind that although the objectives of different individuals within any mentoring scheme may be broadly the same (e.g. to achieve a qualification or to advance their career in a particular direction), their individual way of achieving the objective and, consequently, the help they require may be very different. Therefore, you must clarify the main objective at the start of the relationship and the ways in which the mentee wants you to help them to achieve it.

Ensure that you are clear as to the objectives of the particular relationship and as to those of the mentee.

- The main objective of mentoring is to help another individual to achieve a specific objective.

- You must be very clear about the objective.
- Each individual mentee will have their own ideas about how to achieve their objective and thus the type of help they will require.
- You must ensure that you prepare as much as possible before your first meeting with the mentee in order to ascertain what their objectives are.
- Don't have preconceived ideas of the help you will give to the mentee and how you will do it. Consider different approaches and be prepared to be flexible.
- Remember you are there to help the mentee to achieve their objectives in whatever way is appropriate to them. This may not necessarily be your way.

Be prepared to be flexible in your approach.

OBTAINING BACKGROUND INFORMATION

Before undertaking the mentoring role you will need to do a little research in order to obtain some background information. To build up a relationship you will need to establish a rapport with your mentee, which will be difficult if you are unaware of their background. However it is important that you do not run the risk of damaging the relationship from the start by appearing to pry – by having been too zealous in your research:

Prepare for your first meeting by doing a little background research about your mentee.

- If the mentoring is concerned with professional and/or career issues, knowledge of the mentee's previous academic record and their previous career experience are important.
- The mentee's hobbies and leisure-time activities can be useful subjects as an ice-breaker at initial meetings.
- Try to find out a little about the individual learning style of your mentee.
- Some information about their personality (e.g. whether they are confident, nervous, quiet or shy) will help your approach to them.
- However, you must not appear to be prying too much into their personal lives as it may do more harm than good. Equally, if you go into your first meeting totally ignorant of your mentee's objectives, interests, style and personality, it can give the impression of someone who is not really interested in them.
- You need to strike a balance between showing interest and being overly inquisitive.

> *The more general background information you can obtain about your mentee and their objectives, the quicker you will establish a rapport.*

THE ROLES OF OTHER PARTIES

There will usually be several other parties involved with your mentee. Some of these will have a direct relationship and interest in their work and progress; others will have only a peripheral role. It is important that you establish at the outset who these people are, their roles and how your role of mentor relates to them. This will involve some preparation and research. Job titles are sometimes misleading and it can be dangerous to assume that someone with a title of, say, line manager, office tutor and training manager, carries out the same responsibilities or has identical relationships as others with the same title.

If there is not a mutual understanding of role between you as the mentor and the other parties who come into contact with the mentee, one of two things may happen. Either conflict will arise because you are doing something that someone else considers to be their job, or there will be a problem because you assume that someone else is doing something as part of their role when in fact they are not:

Make sure that you establish at the outset who else has a role to play regarding your mentee and the reasons for the mentoring.

- Make a list of everyone who you think will play a part in helping your mentee to achieve their objectives.
- Write down their titles and a brief description of your perception of what their role would be.
- Try to ascertain if your views of the roles of these individuals coincide with the views of the individuals themselves. It is preferable to do this in advance of the first meeting with your mentee. If this is not possible, you should ensure that you have ways of clearing up any anomalies as soon as possible, preferably by discussing the situation personally with the occupants of the posts concerned. However, in doing this, you should ensure that you do not compromise the confidentiality of your mentoring role.
- Check with your mentee, at the first meeting, that you have covered all the people who may be involved with them and their work and that your understanding of their respective roles is the same as the mentee's.

Try to clarify other people's roles as soon as possible and check your understanding with that of the mentee.

YOUR ROLE IN PREPARING THE MENTEE

No matter how well you prepare yourself for the role of mentor, the process will not succeed unless the mentee has also prepared themselves. If they do not understand what mentoring is all about, have not given some thought to what they want from the mentoring relationship and have few thoughts or ideas on how they would like the process to work, it will be extremely difficult for a successful relationship to be established. Furthermore, there is a great danger that the relationship will become very one-sided and might result in you dictating what should be done rather than working collaboratively with the mentee towards meeting their requirements.

Your role as mentor will be much easier if you have a mentee who understands the purpose of the process, knows what they want to achieve from it and feels confident and at ease with you. Although it is to be hoped that the mentee will receive some form of training before coming into the mentoring scheme, this is by no means certain and it will be in your own interest to ensure that they have prepared themselves properly before the process gets underway:

> *It is in your interest that the mentee prepares themselves.*

- Introduce yourself to them as soon as possible after accepting the role of mentor and before arranging the first meeting.

- Encourage the mentee to think about what they want from the mentoring relationship.
- Encourage them to recognise the real meaning and potential of the relationship.
- Make sure they know how mentoring differs from other personal development tools.
- Make sure that they understand that the sole purpose of the process is to meet their needs and expectations and that they need to communicate these to you.
- Let them know that, although you will probably take the lead in the initial stages, you expect this to change as the relationship grows and that they should eventually lead the process.

Ensure that the mentee understands fully the mentoring process and what your role is.

- Stress that confidentiality is of paramount importance and that you hope that, as the relationship develops, they will feel able to divulge all relevant information about particular issues if they want to get the best from you.
- Clarify and agree your respective understanding of the objectives at an early stage.
- Encourage them to think about the strategy for maintaining contact. Do they want to meet casually

away from a formal setting, or would they prefer more formal arrangements?

- Encourage them to maintain regular contact, even when things are going well.
- Make it clear to them that you think that all issues that affect achievement of their objectives are important, even if they appear trivial at the time.
- Invite them to think seriously about your style and whether it suits them. Make it clear that you will not be upset if they want you to modify your approach.

Make sure they play a part in the strategy for maintaining contact.

- Review with them the information they have received about the process, about your role and about yourself. Don't assume they know everything or that they understand the mentoring scheme.
- Make it clear that you will be happy to give them any additional information that they require.

Get them to think about your role and your style. Encourage them to talk to you about it and not to be afraid to say if it does not suit.

- Ensure that they understand the roles of other parties with whom they come into contact.

THE FIRST MEETING

The first meeting between the mentor and the mentee is vital to the mentoring process and it is important that you prepare for it properly. If you are inadequately prepared there is a great danger that the relationship will get off on the wrong foot, and it would be very difficult to establish a position from which a good and purposeful relationship can grow. Remember that the mentee will probably be wary about the process, especially if they have not had a mentor before and do not fully understand the purpose of the mentoring scheme.

You have to be the one to inspire confidence at the outset and to build up a position of trust so that the mentee will come to look upon you as a 'friend' with whom they can discuss any problems that are affecting the achievement of their objectives. The more quickly you can build up this trust the more successful you are likely to be in establishing a good relationship with them.

However you must not appear to be over-zealous in your approach and, even if you have been quite thorough in your preparation and research, you must not give the impression that you have been delving too deeply into their personal lives. Use your knowledge to produce a balanced approach to the first meeting. The mentee should not be overwhelmed; it is sufficient to demonstrate how well you have prepared and, in so doing, to inspire their confidence:

Make sure you are prepared but adopt a balanced approach to the meeting to build up a rapport.

- Plan your approach to the first meeting to ensure that you start to build up a rapport with your mentee.
- Draw up your own agenda. Include those things you feel you would like to achieve.
- Ensure you have a strategy for setting the future approach for the relationship.
- Make sure you cover such things as:
  - your respective understanding of the mentoring process;
  - the boundaries of the relationship;
  - the roles of other parties;
  - the strategy for maintaining contact; and
  - the mentee's requirements.
- Consider your own approach to these points but be prepared to be flexible in order to accommodate the ideas of the mentee.
- Remember that, if the mentee has prepared themselves for the meeting, they will also have an agenda that will probably differ from yours. Be prepared for that.

Remember the mentee's needs are paramount in the relationship and you must be prepared to be flexible in your approach.

Further details of the process of preparation are included in the following chapter.

IN SUMMARY . . .

- Make sure you understand the mentoring process and in particular your role as mentor.
- Think about the range of issues that might arise and the demands these might create.
- Clarify your objectives.
- Research the background of your mentee, their aims, personality and learning style.
- Establish who else will have a direct relationship with your mentee and clarify their roles.
- Prepare the mentee, ensuring they understand fully the purpose of the mentoring scheme and the benefits they can expect.
- The first meeting with your mentee will set the tone of the future relationship so make sure both of you prepare for it conscientiously.

- Try to build up the confidence of your mentee from the very start.
- Remember that the mentee is the most important person in the relationship, so be flexible wherever possible in order to accommodate their needs.

4

Establishing the Mentoring Relationship

Both you and the mentee will wish to work out whether there is a basis for a good and developmental relationship (i.e. whether you will be able to get on with each other, respect each other and trust each other).

In this chapter:

- setting ground rules
- understanding the nature of the relationship
- setting boundaries
- agreeing strategies for keeping in contact
- matching individual mentoring and learning styles.

For a mentoring relationship to work (as with any relationship) both parties need to understand from the outset the expectations of the other. This will entail agreement on certain ground rules. You will need to encourage the mentee to recognise the potential of a mentoring relationship and the necessity for them to be willing to divulge certain information about relevant matters on a confidential basis. Equally, it is important you ensure that they have complete trust in you to respect such confidences.

It is also important that you agree with the mentee the boundaries of the relationship. You will need to discuss and agree the aspects or subject areas that will be covered, the timescales and any subsequent limitations. It is important they understand and agree these with you at the outset.

Discussing and agreeing your availability and the frequency and method of contact is another important element in establishing your relationship with the mentee. This will include how often you can be available to them, the means by which contact will be made – whether through meetings, by telephone, or by other means – and whether you are prepared to have an 'open door' policy. A feeling of uncertainty in a mentee as to how or where they can contact their mentor can be a disaster for the relationship. A clear strategy for this is therefore essential.

A good rapport between you and your mentee is vital and your individual styles will need to be compatible. If necessary, you may have to modify your individual style in order to meet the mentee's needs.

Self-assessment

- Do you know your 'style' when dealing with other people? Are you able to recognise the needs of the mentee and adapt accordingly?

- Do you find it difficult to build up a rapport easily and quickly with people? If not, how can you do this?

- Can you keep a confidence? Even when you think that by divulging it you can help solve the problem?
- Have you the time and inclination to develop a relationship, even when there appear to be no problems to solve? How do you do this?

SETTING GROUND RULES

It is important that, at the start of a mentoring relationship, both parties appreciate each other's understanding of what they expect from it and how they anticipate it will proceed:

- Set and agree ground rules at the outset. It is important that the respective roles and relationships are known and understood from the start.
- Ensure that the mentee understands their own responsibilities and those of the organisation and line manager.
- Use the first meeting to develop a joint understanding of the relationship and to review your respective backgrounds.

Make sure you know what is expected from the relationship at the outset and agree the ground rules.

UNDERSTANDING THE NATURE OF THE RELATIONSHIP

If a successful rapport is to be established, both you and the mentee must understand how the relationship is to be conducted and what you can expect from each other. In particular, **you** must do the following:

- Encourage the mentee to recognise the real meaning and potential of the mentoring relationship.
- Create an informal atmosphere and put them at their ease.
- Encourage them to be forthcoming about issues that concern them.
- Ensure that anything to be discussed will be fully confidential and nothing will be divulged without their consent.
- Show empathy whenever possible.
- Always remember that mentoring is a two-way process and that the wishes of the mentee are paramount.
- Be prepared to give praise and credit when due.
- Be positive at all times.
- Listen and let the mentee drive the relationship as much as possible. Remember you are there to assist them to achieve their objectives, not to impose your views.
- Don't try to dictate what they should do. Wherever possible let them make their own decisions. Remember that your way of doing things may not necessarily suit

them and that they need to feel comfortable in what they do.

- Wherever practical, have an 'open door' policy and make sure you consider all contact to be important.
- Remember that good relationships are built up by regular contact not by crisis management. Some mentees don't like to bother their mentor unless they think the matter is important. You should discourage this attitude.

You must be positive, must listen, must encourage, but you must not dictate.

A good relationship will only work if both parties play their part and it is important that you understand the mentee's part in the process. In particular, the **mentee** should do the following:

- Be honest with you.
- Be prepared to divulge all relevant information about particular issues.
- Make an effort to get to know you.
- Regard all conversations with you as confidential.
- Ensure they make clear to you what they want from the relationship.
- Not expect you to solve all their problems for them.

- Be flexible in any meeting arrangements.

> *The mentee must be honest and be prepared to act on advice but not expect you to make decisions for them.*

SETTING BOUNDARIES

It is important that both parties accept that there are boundaries to the relationship, which will be governed to a certain extent by the type of mentoring being undertaken. For example, if you are mentoring for a specific task such as the obtaining of a professional qualification, the boundaries will be somewhat narrower than those for more general mentoring.

However, there are some boundaries that should never be crossed. As a **mentor**:

- Don't get personally involved – keep a professional distance.
- Don't raise false hopes by making promises that cannot be fulfilled.
- Accept that both parties have a personal life and learn where the line should be drawn.
- Show you understand the mentee's situation and any problems they might have, but remember that you cannot be an expert in everything and some issues might have to

be referred to someone else, but always with the mentee's consent.

- Make sure you understand the roles of others, for example, tutoring or coaching.
- Make it very clear to the mentee at the outset what you think the boundaries of the relationship are and try to ensure that you understand their boundaries as well. By doing this you will avoid difficulties later on.

> *Don't get into counselling, although a counselling approach may be adopted. Draw the line when it comes to personal involvement and the roles of others. Clear ground rules at the beginning of the relationship will help.*

AGREEING STRATEGIES FOR KEEPING IN CONTACT

Regular contact at all times is essential for a good relationship. A good rapport between the parties can only be built up by talking to each other on a regular basis. Even when things are going well, regular contact should be maintained. Serious problems often start out in a small way, and by talking them over at an early stage, later difficulties can be overcome or avoided altogether.

Each relationship will have different needs for maintaining contact and what suits one relationship will not necessarily work for another. Some mentoring relationships need close proximity for the relationship to work, whilst others will work quite well from a distance. The important thing is to agree a strategy early on with which both parties are happy. Contact doesn't always have to be face to face. Sometimes telephone or e-mail contact can be quite acceptable providing it suits both parties.

> *Good relationships/rapport are built by regular contact.*

Important points to note are as follows:

- Regular contact is the basis of a good working relationship.
- Telephone and e-mail communication can be acceptable in certain circumstances, providing both parties are happy with it and it is backed up with face-to-face contact if necessary.
- The first meeting between the two parties should always be face to face.
- Meetings should be regular and informal. A formal setting can be a bar to building up a good rapport with each other.
- Informal contact (such as having lunch with your mentee or meeting socially) can be a good way of building up a

rapport, but care must be exercised to avoid over-familiarity and over-stepping the agreed boundaries.

- Both parties must be happy with the arrangements and not feel they are inhibiting the relationship.
- Although contact should be regular, some flexibility must be built in.
- Missed or cancelled meetings should be rearranged as soon as possible to avoid the possibility of damaging the relationship.
- Your strategy for keeping in contact should be reviewed on a regular basis to ascertain whether it is still relevant or needs changing.
- An 'open door' policy (accessibility by some means at any time) can only be beneficial.
- Contact should be maintained at all times even when things are going well.
- Both parties should share the responsibility for maintaining contact. In our experience, some mentees don't like to bother their mentor with matters they themselves consider to be trivial. They should be encouraged to discuss these matters.

All methods of contact are important and should be encouraged, but review your contact strategy regularly.

MATCHING INDIVIDUAL MENTORING AND LEARNING STYLES

Not everyone has the same style of working. Whenever possible in a mentoring relationship, it is important that the styles and requirements of the mentor and mentee are matched in a way which enables both parties to get the best from the relationship.

If the relationship is not working because there is a clash of styles, this doesn't necessarily mean that someone has failed. However it is important to be honest about the situation and you should be prepared to modify your style to suit the mentee. If this is not possible it is preferable to sever the relationship rather than have it continue in an unsatisfactory manner.

Try to ascertain whether your style and that of the mentee are compatible and if not you should try to modify your style accordingly.

All styles should reflect a positive attitude. However, the following individual points should be considered.

For **you**:

- What attributes you can best offer to the mentee?
- What is your mentoring style? Is it an active one (i.e. are you someone who challenges, questions, pushes as appropriate)? Or is it a passive one (i.e. someone who is

a good sounding board for ideas and is able to lead the mentee into making their own decisions)? Think about your own style and be prepared to change if necessary.

- Are you willing to share your experiences and approaches?
- Are you willing and able to adapt your style to meet the requirements of the mentee?

> *You should make a list of the attributes you think you can bring to the relationship.*

For the **mentee**:

- Find out what they expect from you.
- Do they like someone who will push them or someone who is just prepared to listen and offer advice from time to time?
- Do they want someone to use as a resource (i.e. to help with introductions and networking)?
- Do they want someone whom they can look to as a role model?
- Do they just need someone who will encourage and bolster their confidence from time to time?

Find out what the mentee wants from the relationship and try to match them with your style.

If possible, the individual styles of mentor and mentee should be considered when mentors are being appointed. However, this is not always possible as, for example, the styles and personalities of new employees might not be known.

The first few meetings between you amd your mentee should soon indicate any problems with styles and, if relevant, you should consider whether you are able to modify your style to accommodate the requirements of the mentee. If not you should be honest and ask that another, better suited, mentor should be appointed.

Try to ascertain if styles are compatible at an early stage and, if not, be prepared to modify or end the relationship.
Be honest. Recognise if there is a problem and act early to rectify it.

IN SUMMARY . . .

- Make sure both you and the mentee understand the nature of the relationship and the role of the mentor and set the ground rules at the start.

- The requirements of the mentee are paramount and the nature of the relationship should reflect this.
- You should listen, encourage, give advice but never dictate.
- All discussions should be confidential. This confidence should never be breached without permission of the other party (unless an illegal act is being carried out), even if doing so can solve a problem.
- The relationship should be conducted in an informal atmosphere and should never be confrontational.
- Wherever possible the mentee should drive the relationship, as it is the fulfilment of their requirements and objectives that is important.
- Ensure that both you and your mentee recognise the boundaries and do not get personally involved or impinge on the roles of third parties (e.g. line managers).
- Regular contact helps to build a rapport and is the basis of a good relationship.
- Make sure that the format of all contact is comfortable to both you and the mentee.
- Have a strategy for keeping in touch and stick to it even when everything is going well and there are no problems. Remember, praise and credit for things going well are just as important as solving problems.
- If you have to cancel or miss an appointment rearrange it as soon as possible and apologise if necessary.

- Individual styles will differ and a good match is important if the relationship is to be successful.
- Try to assess your style to see if it fits with the requirement of the other party.
- Be honest and, if there is a clash of styles, be prepared to do something about it.
- Review the relationship on a regular basis and be prepared to change things if necessary.

5

The Mentoring Process

Mentoring is essentially a practical exercise and you will find that your skill as a mentor will get better with practice. No two situations are identical and what works within one relationship will not necessarily work for another. There are very few instances when you can apply a standard answer to any particular problem, and thus there are no right or wrong solutions you will be able to apply universally. Nevertheless, there are certain good practices that will help you to tackle the role in a positive manner. Likewise, there are several bad practices to be avoided.

In this chapter:

- mentoring meetings
- planning the logistics of meetings
- dealing with issues
- using networking to help your mentee
- maintaining contact
- taking into account external relationships.

In order to undertake the role of mentor you will need to communicate with your mentee on an ongoing and regular basis. The way in which you prepare for and carry out mentoring meetings can have an important bearing on the relationship. Your approach to the meetings and the logistics used to set the scene for them can affect the way in which your mentee views you and the mentoring process. You will need to consider how to deal with issues that will arise. These may be work related, personal, technical or professional, and each type may need a different approach.

One of the most important ways in which you can assist your mentee to achieve their objectives is by networking. It is extremely unlikely that you will be able to give help and advice on all the issues that will arise. However, your experience may well have enabled you to build up a network of contacts that you can use to increase the options open to you. You can also use such networking to enable the mentee to develop and widen their own contacts.

You will find that, if you are to build up a good relationship with your mentee to such an extent that they will come to trust you, you will need to find ways of maintaining contact with them at all times, not just when there are problems. The ways in which you do this will vary and must be in a style that is comfortable for both parties.

No matter how much you work at the mentoring process there will often be times when conflict will arise with third parties who also have a relationship with your mentee. For you to be successful you will have to learn how to deal with these external relationships. Both you and your mentee will have to understand the roles of these other people and you will need to be able to deal with any circumstances that arise without breaking the rules of confidentiality or having an adverse effect on a situation.

Self-asssessment

- Have you the time and desire to prepare adequately for meetings with your mentee?
- Have you sufficient experience and contacts to enable you to carry out the role in a practical way, which will enable you to give your mentee the confidence to make the relationship work?
- Are you sufficiently tactful to be able to deal with other people who have a relationship with your mentee?
- Do you feel able to adapt your style in communicating with your mentee in order to ensure that you can build up their confidence in you to maintain contact at all times, not just when there are problems?
- Would you feel comfortable in dealing with issues of a personal nature if they were affecting the mentee's ability to achieve their objectives?

MENTORING MEETINGS

In order to be successful as a mentor you will need to meet with your mentee on a regular basis. The meetings do not necessarily have to be formal; indeed, it is usually better to create an informal atmosphere in order to establish rapport and to put the mentee at ease. However, just because the meeting is not conducted in a formal way does not mean you should not prepare well in advance, so make sure you allow sufficient time at the meeting to deal with all the expected issues. Most importantly, don't underestimate the time required for preparation.

> *Prepare thoughly for all meetings and ensure you allow sufficient time to deal with all the issues that are likely to arise.*

Try to put the mentee at ease by raising issues of common interest and encourage them to do most of the talking. Although you should have a structure/plan for your meeting (which should include any points that you wish to raise), make sure it is flexible and be prepared to vary your plan to fit in with anything the mentee might bring up. Prepare for the meeting from the mentee's perspective as well as your own. Don't assume that your priorities are the same as theirs.

If you have an indication that your mentee might have a problem, either because of something you have heard or some indication from them that all is not well, try to plan for how you will tackle this before the meeting. They might not be prepared to divulge everything and you will need to construct any questions carefully in a manner that will protect confidentiality. You must encourage them to talk to you willingly about any problem and not to push them if they are reluctant to discuss certain issues.

Look and listen for signs that indicate there may be a problem.

Make sure you include in your agenda any outstanding issues from previous discussions. In particular, confirm actions taken, review the current situation and agree further actions. Make sure you review the arrangements for meetings and, if the initial arrangements don't appear to be working, change them. Arrange for them to be mutually convenient. If necessary you should arrange to meet out of hours in an informal setting. This can be particularly useful if confidential matters are likely to arise. Most importantly, make sure both of you are happy with the way in which the discussions take place and encourage the mentee to take an active part in the arrangements for meetings.

Be prepared to change arrangements to suit both parties.

At the first meeting discuss the manner in which future meetings will take place (i.e. whether formally or informally) and where, and be prepared to adapt the arrangements as the relationship develops.

PLANNING THE LOGISTICS OF YOUR MEETINGS

Think very carefully about the logistics of your meetings. How you set them up and the surroundings in which you hold them can affect the way in which your mentee views both you and the whole mentoring process.

Always remember that your role as a mentor is to assist your mentee to achieve certain objectives and to help them to do so in a manner with which they are happy. If you meet with them in a confrontational way (e.g. across a desk with you on one side and them on the other), there may be connotations of a formal boss/subordinate relationship. This may make the mentee suspicious of the whole process. What you need to do is create an atmosphere where they feel they can chat to you and, if necessary, talk openly about any problems without the fear of being criticised.

Create a friendly location that is conducive to building up a rapport.

Always try to meet in an area where confidentiality can be maintained. If the meeting is to be in the workplace don't arrange it in an open office with other employees and possibly colleagues present and within earshot. Use an independent office or a coffee lounge away from the normal working area. If you meet in an office try to arrange the seating informally without the constraints of an office desk between you. Make sure, however, that there are facilities for any paperwork to be spread out if necessary. Don't expect either of you to sit with papers on your knee trying to write and make notes at the same time. If you do have to hold the meeting in an office with a desk or table, try sitting on the same side to avoid the confrontational approach. Whatever arrangements you have, try to ensure both of you are comfortable with them. Don't assume the mentee is – ask them and change if necessary.

DEALING WITH ISSUES

A whole range of issues can arise during your relationship, not only related directly to the main purpose for which you are mentoring, but also including personal, professional and technical issues. Some will concern other parties associated with the mentee. You will have to learn how to deal with these if you are to be successful. Much of the way in which you will deal with such issues will only come about with experience as you build up a rapport with your mentee and each circumstance is likely to be different. However, there are some basic guidelines that are useful to follow:

- Try to agree the boundaries of the relationship at the outset.
- Don't get involved in personal issues unless they have a significant effect on the relationship as a whole.
- Don't try to be 'all things to all people'. You can't solve all the problems and if you try you run the risk of destroying the mentee's confidence in you.
- Know your own limitations and try to stick to them.
- Listen and suggest possible solutions to be considered, but try to encourage the mentee to find their own solution if possible.

- Don't impose solutions.
- Don't stray into the roles of others. Be clear where to draw the line and when to suggest they talk to some other person (e.g. line manager, trainer, etc.).
- Be honest and be prepared to say 'I don't know' if that is the case.
- Don't rush in with a solution until you are aware of all the facts and don't assume there is only one solution. Try to offer alternative ways of dealing with the problem.
- Don't get emotionally involved.

Above all, you should listen, be positive and encourage the mentee to work out their own solutions. Don't impose your ideas, know your limitations and don't try to do other people's jobs.

USING NETWORKING TO HELP YOUR MENTEE

It is unlikely you will be able support your mentee entirely from your own experiences and knowledge. It can be dangerous if you try to do so as on occasions you are almost certain to fail. This may result in the mentee losing confidence in you and in the process generally. However it may well be that you have built up a network of colleagues and acquaintances who are able to help in certain areas which are outside your field of work experience.

You should use these networks to help your mentee when such an issue arises in order to try to arrive at the best solution. Technical issues, in particular, may well be best dealt with by putting the mentee in touch with someone known to you who has the skills and knowledge to deal with the problem. For mentees who are studying and facing a problem with a particular subject, it is sometimes advantageous for them to discuss the situation with a peer who is doing the same course or someone who has recently completed the course. If you know such an individual within your network, putting the mentee in touch may be the answer to their problem.

Equally important is helping the mentee to build up their own network. This could take many years if left to their own devices, but with your help a network of useful contacts can be built up very quickly and can be an invaluable aid to their development.

Use your networks to help your mentee and help your mentee to build up their own networks.

MAINTAINING CONTACT

Whereas regular meetings are the main routes by which progress and action in the mentoring process occur, it is also very important to maintain contact on an informal basis between meetings. Mentoring is very much about building up a relationship and developing rapport and trust between the two parties. Normally, it will not be too successful if communications are limited to regular meetings and discussions planned to deal with progress and issues in a formal way. This may work up to a point but, if the relationship is to be really strong and meaningful, the mentee has to feel they can consider their mentor as a friend with whom they can communicate on a regular and informal basis. However this has to be in a way that suits both parties and with which they are comfortable.

At the outset of the relationship both mentor and mentee should think about how they are going to maintain contact. Do they want a total 'open door' policy in which the mentee is free to contact the mentor at any time? This may mean at home as well as in the workplace. Do they want to meet occasionally on an informal basis in a social situation?

It is important that the mentor encourages the mentee to stay in touch at all times, when things are going well as well as when there are problems. Experience shows that many major problems could have been avoided if regular communications had been maintained.

Stay in touch on a regular basis even when things are going well.

It is usually in these informal meetings that relationships are built up which help to solve or even avoid difficult problems later on.

TAKING INTO ACCOUNT EXTERNAL RELATIONSHIPS

You must never lose sight of the fact that your mentee will have several other people with whom they have some sort of professional relationship. It is important that you establish who these people are and the extent of their relationship. Discuss with your mentee at your first meeting the boundaries with regard to your role, the roles of others and how far you are prepared to go into areas these other people cover. Because, as we have said, your relationship with the mentee should be strictly confidential, you should never discuss issues relating to them with other parties without their consent. It is a good idea, with your mentee's approval, to meet with the people with whom they have a professional relationship at the start of the mentoring process to explain your role and to avoid misunderstanding.

When an issue arises that concerns one of the other parties, you should ensure you do not give conflicting advice or that you interfere with someone else's role. If your advice is in danger of conflicting with another person's role, try to get your mentee to tackle it with that person first. Only if this is not possible or the mentee is very reluctant to do so should you get involved and even then you should obtain your mentee's permission to discuss the situation with the other person if necessary. If you cannot solve a problem without discussing it with the other person, and it is likely to cause a conflict, don't do so.

Don't give conflicting advice and don't do other people's jobs.

IN SUMMARY . . .

- The way in which you prepare and plan for regular meetings can have an important bearing on the relationship.
- Create an informal atmosphere in order to establish rapport and put the mentee at ease.
- Make sure you include in your 'agenda' any outstanding issues from previous discussions and any subsequent actions.
- Consider your mentee's perspective as well as your own; don't assume your priorities are the same.
- Try to encourage the mentee to lead the discussions.
- Think very carefully about the logistics of your meeting and, in particular, the venue and the way in which furniture is arranged to create the right atmosphere.
- If the initial arrangements don't appear to be working, change them. If necessary, agree to meet out of hours in an informal location.
- Agree boundaries, within which you feel comfortable, for dealing with issues.
- Don't try to be all things to all people and know your limitations.
- Listen and suggest possible solutions. Remember it is far better if the mentee makes the decision rather than having it imposed.

- Be positive, be honest, but don't get emotionally involved.
- Use your own contacts and networks to help.
- Encourage and help the mentee to develop their own networks.
- Think about and discuss early in the relationship the ways in which you are going to maintain contact other than through regular meetings.
- Make sure that whatever arrangements you make are acceptable to both parties.
- All contact is important and is just as necessary when things are going well as well as when there are problems.
- A good relationship will enable problems to be sorted out before they become major ones. Good regular contact will assist this process.
- Establish any external professional relationships with your mentee at the outset and make sure you do not conflict with their roles.
- If possible and with the agreement of your mentee, establish contact with other people who have a professional relationship with your mentee and explain your role to them.
- Whatever you do, don't give conflicting advice. If you can't get the mentee to discuss the situation with the third person and you can't get their agreement to talk to them yourself, leave it alone or you are likely to do more harm than good.

6

Ending the Mentoring Relationship

You will need to give some consideration to how the relationship will develop and to how and when it will end. You will need to distinguish between when it has reached the end of its natural life (i.e. when it has achieved its objectives) and when it needs to end because it isn't working as originally planned. It is important that, if the relationship is to come to an end, for whatever reason, it is done in such a way that it enables the mentee to move on and not to feel that the process has been a failure.

In this chapter:

- agreeing the objectives
- planning your strategy in advance
- recognising when the relationship is not working
- setting the 'end date'
- recommendations for a continuing mentoring arrangement.

When becoming a mentor you will have agreed objectives with the mentee and any others involved in the process so that there were no misunderstandings about the limitations of your own involvement and when you expected, in terms of achievement of these objectives, the relationship to come to an end. In planning your strategy for achieving the objectives you should have included review points along the way in order to assess 'how you are doing'. Regular reviews should have been built in to give your mentee an opportunity to assess how the process is going from their standpoint.

Not all mentoring relationships will work as expected and you must be prepared to recognise when it is not working and do something about it. If necessary, end the relationship in an amicable fashion and make alternative arrangements. It is important that both parties in the mentoring process are clear as to the circumstances under which the arrangements will come to an end. Setting the 'end date' as early as possible will avoid any unnecessary difficulties when the time comes to end the relationship. This 'end date' may be in fact when a specific event or circumstance has occurred rather than a specific date.

Whenever the relationship comes to an end, consideration should be given to what, if anything, should replace it. It may well be that the original objectives have not been achieved and you cannot take matters any further, or it may be they have been achieved and that there are further stages for the mentee to undertake which are not within your scope. Whatever the reasons, you should assist in making arrangements for any continuing mentoring to be undertaken.

Self-assessment

- Are you able to focus on the objectives without getting side-tracked?
- Do you think you will be able to recognise when the relationship is not working, and would you be willing to do something about it?
- Are you able to 'let go' at the appropriate time?
- Will you be able to recognise when you have reached the limit of your capabilities with regard to the help you can give to your mentee?

AGREEING THE OBJECTIVES

At the start of the mentoring relationship you will have agreed objectives with your mentee. You should also have made it clear to them at the outset that when these objectives have been achieved it will probably mean that the relationship will come to an end, and that any further mentoring that is required will probably have to be carried out by someone else:

- At the outset, you will have agreed with your mentee the objectives you wished to achieve and the limitations, if any, on the help you were able to give.
- You will have ensured that the mentee recognised that there would be a definite end to the relationship at some time in the future and that this would probably occur when the agreed objectives had been achieved.

- You will have made sure that you have a methodology for assessing these objectives and what the success criteria for them will be.
- You will also have agreed with the mentee what you will do if, at any time, you feel unable to help with the achievement of the agreed objectives and agree with them the point at which it might be desirable to change mentors.

PLANNING YOUR STRATEGY IN ADVANCE

When writing your initial strategy you should have a clear idea of when the mentoring relationship will come to an end. This will be either on fulfilment of the initial objectives or when, for whatever reason, you feel that you can no longer carry out the role successfully. It is important that you set your own criteria for success, having regard to your own limitations in what you can offer in terms of time, commitment and personal qualities:

- Plan your own strategy for dealing with the relationship.
- Set realistic goals for achievement of objectives.
- Set your own standards for deciding whether or not the relationship is working as planned.
- Set yourself dates for reviewing the process and, if it isn't working, consider what you can do about it.
- Make sure you plan in advance for ending the relationship and, if necessary, how you can help to transfer the process to someone else.
- Consider the mentee's style and ambitions and be

prepared to adapt to them if necessary, but don't try to continue if you feel uncomfortable with the situation.

If possible, plan for any transitional process when your relationship with the mentee comes to an end.

RECOGNISING WHEN THE RELATIONSHIP IS NOT WORKING

One of the most common failures in mentoring schemes arises when relationships continue even though it is obvious that they are not working. This can be for many reasons and are not usually the fault of either party. It is often simply a case of a failure to recognise that things have changed since the original relationship was set up. Individual aims and objectives change, styles differ and, sometimes, the circumstances of either yourself or the mentee alter with the result that what was once considered feasible can no longer work as envisaged.

- Review your strategy at regular intervals.
- Consider whether or not objectives and criteria are being met.
- If circumstances of either party change, consider if you can still give the quality of mentoring required by your mentee.
- Ensure that you and your mentee are comfortable with the relationship.

- Be honest and don't try to continue with something that is not working.
- Encourage your mentee to be honest with you and to tell you if they are unhappy with the relationship.

> *If circumstances of either party change, consider the effect this might have on the relationship. Be honest and don't keep things going for the sake of appearances.*

SETTING THE END DATE

Ascertain right at the start of the relationship the circumstances under which the relationship will end. This can either be a specific date, the completion of a specific objective or objectives or when circumstances are such as to prevent the relationship from achieving any significant progress. A properly thought-out exit strategy will reduce many of the difficulties that can arise out of the ending of a relationship which, in some cases, can be quite traumatic.

> *If possible, try to agree at the beginning the point at which the relationship will end.*

- If the relationship has been set up to achieve specific measurable objectives such as the gaining of a professional qualification or to oversee someone through a period of transition with a clearly definable end date, this should be recognised and should signal quite clearly the end of the mentoring relationship.
- Any further mentoring that may be required should be the subject of a new agreement and, probably, a new mentor.
- The more difficult end dates to determine are those where the objectives are not so clearly defined. These might be concerned with general career development, or a new venture that does not have a specific end date. It is important that these are recognised and that some point is identified within the strategy at which progress can be reviewed. At this stage, if insufficient progress has been made, either the relationship should end or an extended period agreed to enable the mentee to move to a further measurable stage in their development.

Review the progress being made on a regular basis and amend the end date if necessary in the light of the reviews.

- The other point at which a relationship can be ended is if, for any reason, the relationship is not working and is failing to achieve what it set out to do. This can be difficult to determine, especially if insufficient thought has been given in the planning strategy to the criteria by which the success of the relationship will be measured. Even when such criteria have been established, it is important that they are reviewed on a regular basis.

- Both parties should agree at the outset the circumstances under which they will determine whether or not the relationship is working.

Ensure that you agree the circumstances under which you will end the relationship if it is not working to the satisfaction of both parties.

RECOMMENDATIONS FOR A CONTINUING MENTORING ARRANGEMENT

The end of your relationship with a mentee does not necessarily mean that no further mentoring is required. It may be that the relationship has come to an end before the original objectives have been achieved, or a point may have been reached at which mentoring skills and attributes other than yours are required. Even with the most successful mentoring arrangements there may well come a point where the mentee's development may have taken a different direction or some new and different objectives are required. Whatever the reasons for the ending of your involvement, you can play an important role in making recommendations for any continuing mentoring of your mentee:

> *When the relationship is about to come to an end, give some thought as to any recommendations you can make for continuing the process – in the light of your experiences.*

- If the relationship is to end because you are unable to continue for any reason, make sure your experiences, and particularly any problems and difficulties you have encountered are made known to whoever has the task of appointing a successor. If, for any reason, the relationship hasn't worked it is important that lessons are learned so that mistakes are not repeated. Any information you pass on must be positive and given in confidence.

- If the relationship is ending because it has achieved its objectives you should be able to make recommendations about any known future mentoring requirements. Knowledge of what has been learned from your involvement as mentor, and perhaps your opinion of the qualities and experience to be looked for in whoever might mentor the next stage of the mentee's development, can be invaluable.

- Make sure you discuss with your mentee the things that have been learned from the relationship that will be helpful in the future. If possible, offer some reassurance that you will be willing to give any help and advice on any past problems, but make it clear you consider that your mentoring relationship is over. Don't let it drag on, and emphasise that someone else should cover any future mentoring requirements.

End the relationship amicably and pass on any learning points.

IN SUMMARY . . .

- Agree the objectives and limits of the mentoring process at the outset.
- Agree the criteria by which you will assess the success of each objective.
- Plan your strategy for the relationship at the start and try to establish when the end date (or event) will be.
- Set yourself goals and standards and review them on a regular basis.
- Amend the end date if necessary in the light of your review.
- Make sure you include an exit strategy in your overall plan.
- Plan for any transitional process if necessary when the relationship comes to an end.
- Consider the circumstances under which the relationship might have to end prematurely.
- Be honest and end the relationship if it isn't working. Don't keep it going when it isn't achieving the criteria set.

- Pass on any constructive comments based on your experiences to both the mentee and any other party involved in the process so as to aid any future mentoring arrangements.
- Don't breach confidentiality.

7

Benefits and Pitfalls

In undertaking the role of mentor it will be helpful for you to give some thought to the benefits that both you and your mentee are likely to get from taking part in the process. When agreeing your objectives you should also consider the likely benefits for each of you and plan to review their achievement as your relationship progresses. However, although mentoring is a relatively straightforward process, sometimes things can go wrong. Therefore, it is of equal importance for you to be aware of the pitfalls that might arise if you do not undertake your role in a systematic and purposeful way.

In this chapter:

- considering the benefits to you as a mentor
- the benefits to the mentee
- the pitfalls that may arise
- avoiding the pitfalls.

If your mentoring relationship is to be successful and both you and the mentee are to achieve your agreed objectives, you should give some thought at an early stage to the expected benefits to you as a mentor as well as to the benefits to the mentee. As with any process, however, things can go wrong and pitfalls may arise. It is important, therefore, that you try to anticipate them and consider how you can plan to meet them.

Self-assessment

- Are you aware of the benefits that both you as mentor and your mentee can expect through working together in a mentoring relationship?
- Can you plan with your mentee to achieve them?
- Can you anticipate the pitfalls that might arise during a mentoring relationship?
- Can you view likely pitfalls positively and plan to try to ensure they do not arise?

CONSIDERING THE BENEFITS TO YOU AS MENTOR

Through our involvement in mentoring schemes, in our research and in running workshops we have found that there is a lot of fulfilment to be gained from undertaking the role of mentor. Much of this benefit is of a personal nature, concerned with the mentor's status and reputation within the organisation, but there are professional and personal benefits as well.

The benefits to you as the mentor include the following:

- **An opportunity to further your own personal development**. In dealing with your mentee, and fulfilling your part of your contract with them, you will need to use many of the skills already referred to in Chapter 2. It is possible that some of these skills may be new to you and so the development and use of them could be a good development opportunity for you.

- **A chance for you to update your own ideas and techniques**. This might be especially so in a number of mentoring roles. If you are undertaking the role of professional qualification mentor or vocational qualification mentor, you will need to be up to date with the current syllabus of the professional institute for whose qualification the mentee is studying or, in the case of a vocational qualification mentor, the requirements of the qualification awarding body for the acquisition of experience by the mentee and for the assembly of evidence for their portfolio. The role of training mentor will also enable you to keep abreast with current procedures and techniques within your organisation. This might also be applicable in general mentoring.

- **An opportunity to participate in your organisation's training and development strategies**. Where mentoring has been set up formally as part of your organisation's training and development strategy, you will have a heightened opportunity to participate in that.

- **Increased peer recognition and network of contacts**. If you are acting as mentor to a colleague whose programme requires you to facilitate access for them to levels of management higher than your own, the task of arranging that and the contacts consequently made can enhance your reputation at higher levels and within the organisation as a whole.

- **Increased personal reputation and job satisfaction**. Just being involved as mentor can bring its own rewards. The fact that you have been deemed to be the right type of person to be selected can enhance your personal reputation. The task of being involved in helping a colleague or another person to achieve their career or personal objectives can be invigorating and can create an enhanced sense of purpose and a sense of achievement.
- **The satisfaction of seeing your advice being put into effect with good results**. Mentoring can be a good morale booster for the mentor. It is always satisfying to see your own ideas and advice put into effect and achieving the expected results.
- **The mentee brings a new outlook to the organisation by challenging established procedures and values**. An enthusiastic and imaginative mentee can often bring a fresh approach to existing values, processes and ideas. In our experience we have seen a number of such cases where entire organisations have benefited from the adoption of new policies or ideas recommended by students or trainees from projects undertaken as part of their development programmes and where the mentors have recommended the outcomes for implementation.
- **Something else for you to include on your CV**. Personal development can be an important factor when applying for a new job. The fact that you have been a mentor might be an advantage.

THE BENEFITS TO THE MENTEE

Mentoring is intended primarily to help the mentee. If they are to achieve all the benefits, it is essential that they are briefed adequately, as detailed earlier. As a mentor, you will play a significant part in that. Your role will be to discuss with your mentee the nature and purpose of the scheme and the likely benefits they can expect, some of which are as follows:

- Mentees, particularly those who are trainees or other new employees, are able to adapt quickly and to find their feet within the organisation.
- A ready, impartial and trusted source of advice is available to them in the person of the mentor.
- Through the mentor they will have a ready communication link with all levels within the organisation.
- The mentor can be a role model, available to help them focus their career aspirations and to work towards their objectives.
- If they are undertaking a formal training or development programme, the mentor is a source of help who understands the requirements and expectations of their programme.
- The mentor, through their own experience, is able to help them to understand and to get to grips with the structures of the organisation.
- The mentee can gain a higher profile within the organisation through the encouragement and support of the mentor.

- By observing the mentor, they can gain an insight into the workings of the organisation.

THE PITFALLS THAT MAY ARISE

The benefits of mentoring will not be achieved, and may even be negated, if you do not follow the rules we have suggested in earlier chapters. There is a real danger of this, particularly if you:

- Do not give enough time to the mentoring task.
- Adopt a casual approach to your meetings or other forms of contact with your mentee and change them unilaterally without good reason and do not make further arrangements immediately.
- Appear to be disorganised and ill-prepared for your meetings with the mentee.
- Do not take the trouble to understand the needs and expectations of the mentee.
- Try to be nice to everyone and to satisfy their needs – in fact, to be 'all things to all people'.
- Do not *listen* to what the mentee is saying to you.
- Do not keep a professional distance and become too familiar with the mentee and personally involved with them.
- Adopt a patronising attitude and do not treat the mentee as an adult.
- Do not carry out what you have undertaken and, in effect, do not fulfil your part of the bargain.

- Overstep the boundaries – for example, by straying into tutoring or direct training.

AVOIDING THE PITFALLS

The responsibility for maintaining the mentoring relationship rests with you as the mentor. If you do not make every effort to do so, some of the pitfalls might occur. It is important, therefore, to give some consideration to avoiding them. Here are a few suggestions:

- Do not promise what you are unable to deliver.
- Always do what you have promised within the time agreed.
- Don't let the relationship break down through lack of or infrequent contact.
- Bear in mind that you can't solve all the mentee's problems at one meeting.
- When meeting the mentee, don't talk too much and don't be dictatorial.
- Always give the mentee the opportunity to speak and listen to what they are saying.
- Stick to your mentoring role and don't stray into management.
- Finally, and above all, maintain confidentiality and don't talk to others without the mentee's consent.

> *Make sure that you try to anticipate all likely pitfalls and plan to meet them.*

IN SUMMARY . . .

- Make sure you are clear in your mind about the benefits you will get from acting as a mentor:
  - an opportunity to be involved in the development of another person;
  - an opportunity to update your own professional skills and knowledge;
  - a challenge and, if you are successful in the role, a sense of achievement;
  - enhanced status within your organisation; and
  - a chance to be part of your organisation's formal training and development strategies.
- Consider, also, the benefits to the mentee:
  - a more speedy achievement of their objectives and, if they are new, assimilation into the organisation;
  - with your help, a ready communication link with all organisational levels;
  - help and guidance is available with interpreting and achieving the expectations of any development programme they may be following; and

- a higher profile within the organisation.

◆ Anticipate the pitfalls that might arise:

- devoting insufficient time to your role;
- adopting a casual approach to the relationship with your mentee and the arrangements made for your discussions;
- not listening to what they are saying;
- not doing what you have agreed to do; and
- exceeding your role as mentor by straying into the responsibilities of other parties and thus creating poor relationships with them.

◆ Plan to try to avoid likely pitfalls:

- only promise to do what you know you can deliver and do so within the agreed timescale;
- maintain regular contact with your mentee and do not vary arrangements for contact without good cause;
- don't talk too much at meetings;
- know your role and the limits of your involvement and do not exceed them; and
- maintain confidentiality.

8

Getting Started

Having looked at the nature and purpose of mentoring and its many applications, you will now want to think seriously about getting started. Whatever type of mentoring you may become involved in, the basic principles and the stages of the mentoring process are the same. This chapter summarise the process you need to go through in order to get started.

In this chapter:

- what you can bring to the mentoring role
- what you can gain from becoming a mentor
- preparing yourself and your mentee
- approaching the task methodically
- periodically reviewing the process and the relationship.

Having decided that you wish to take on the role of mentor, on what you can bring to the role and having quantified the benefits you expect for both yourself and your mentee, you should then undertake the necessary preparation. Having got started, you need to approach the task in a methodical and systematic way and provide an opportunity to review the process periodically with your mentee so as to ensure that your respective objectives continue to be met.

Self-assessment

- Are you sufficiently aware of the nature and purpose of mentoring so as to be able to quantify the benefits that both you and a mentee would gain from working together in a mentoring relationship?
- Can you prepare both yourself and your mentee for the process so that you can embark upon it with mutual confidence and trust?
- Will you have the time and commitment to undertake the role?
- Can you develop the necessary mentoring relationships with sufficient empathy and understanding, and will you be able to review, with your mentee, the objectives and process on a periodic basis?
- Do you want to do it?

WHAT YOU CAN BRING TO THE MENTORING ROLE

To succeed in your mentoring role you must be clear about why you want to do it and what you are going to get from it. There are many reasons for undertaking the role:

- You are fully qualified in your field and wish to help someone who is aspiring to achieve the same level of competence.
- You wish to use your experience and network of contacts to benefit another person.

- You are interested in developing or enhancing your skills, particularly in staff development.
- You have been asked to become a mentor because you are regarded as having the knowledge, experience and personal qualities to do it well.

In all these circumstances it would be helpful both to yourself and your potential mentee for you to consider, before accepting the role, what *you* think you can bring to it and the benefits that are likely to result.

WHAT YOU CAN GAIN FROM BECOMING A MENTOR

This is an important question because, unless you are certain about the benefits *you* are going to get, it is likely you may not go into the role with enthusiasm. As mentioned in Chapter 7, there are many personal benefits as well as some related to your own status and career development. You will certainly get the opportunity of practising and developing a number of personal skills, such as listening, communicating, influencing and fact-finding. Depending upon the nature of the mentoring you are doing, you might also get the opportunity of updating your professional knowledge and of enhancing your personal status by gaining access to higher levels within the organisation.

By thinking about your reasons for wishing to become a mentor and what you expect to get from undertaking the role you will go a long way towards quantifying just what you can bring to a mentoring relationship.

PREPARING YOURSELF AND YOUR MENTEE

Preparing yourself

The following are ways in which you can prepare yourself for the role of mentor:

- Clarify whether your role will be part of any formal mentoring scheme within the organisation and how you will relate to the scheme co-ordinator.
- Consider the type of mentoring you will be undertaking and the likely needs of a mentee.
- Find out all you can about the person who is to be your mentee.
- Contact others who have any involvement with your mentee and discuss with them your role as mentor.
- Think about the benefits you can gain from being a mentor.
- Make sure that you understand the commitment you will have to make and give some thought to the likely objectives and boundaries of the relationship.

Preparing your mentee

The following are ways in which you can prepare your mentee for the mentoring process:

- As soon as you know who your mentee will be, make initial contact with them.
- Make sure that they understand fully the purpose of the mentoring scheme, your role within it and how it relates to other staff development tools.

- Discuss with them the purpose and extent of your mentoring relationship and the time period over which it will continue.
- Agree the means and frequency of contact and the arrangements for your first meeting, including an informal agenda.

APPROACHING THE TASK METHODICALLY

Prepare yourself logistically:

- Arrange a suitable time and venue for your first meeting, ensuring that it takes place in a private, yet comfortable, setting.
- Make sure that you have planned sufficient time in your diary. It would look bad if, at the first meeting, you have to cut things short to dash to another appointment.
- Ensure that you draw up an agenda for dealing with all the issues both of you wish to discuss.

During your mentoring meetings:

- Adopt a welcoming attitude and encourage the mentee to discuss openly and confidentially, matters relating to their development.
- Try to stick to the agenda you have agreed previously with the mentee, but be sufficiently flexible to deal with anything else they may wish to raise.
- Don't get involved in personal issues unless they have a significant effect on the mentoring relationship.

- Make sure that you *listen* and are *seen* to listen.
- Don't try to solve all the mentee's problems – know your limitations and function within them.
- Don't be afraid to say 'I don't know'.
- Don't impose solutions on your mentee – encourage them to consider the pros and cons of possible alternatives and then to decide for themselves.
- Use your networks to help them, and encourage them to develop their own.
- Periodically, ensure that both of you are happy with the content and conduct of the meetings.
- Discuss and agree the agenda and your objectives for the next meeting.
- As the time approaches when your mentoring relationship is to end, begin to implement your exit strategy. This might also be necessary if it appears to both of you that the relationship is breaking down and that your respective objectives are not being met.

Between meetings:

- Make sure that you take action on all the points that you have agreed.
- Keep in informal contact with your mentee, either by brief telephone calls to check everything is satisfactory or by a brief chat if your paths happen to cross.
- Do not alter the arrangements for your next meeting unless it is absolutely essential to do so. If it is necessary,

explain the reason and make alternative arrangements as soon as possible.

PERIODICALLY REVIEWING THE PROCESS AND THE RELATIONSHIP

At periodic intervals you should also carry out a review of the process and the relationship to date. Together with your mentee you should consider:

- whether the original objectives are being met within a timescale that is acceptable to both of you;
- any circumstances that have arisen that have changed the original plan;
- whether you are staying within the agreed boundaries; and
- whether both of you feel happy with the manner in which the relationship is being conducted.

Having carried out the review you should amend the strategy if necessary and consider if the relationship is still appropriate. **Don't keep a relationship going just for the sake of appearances. If it is not working or no longer appropriate, implement your exit strategy**.

Finally, to be involved as a mentor can be as exciting and rewarding as it is fulfilling. You have the opportunity to take part in the development and progression of another person and of seeing your advice put into good effect. It can also be an opportunity for furthering your own personal development.

However, as with every other management or development technique, it doesn't always come right at the start – to be a good mentor needs practice. In the final chapter we have included a number of case studies. These are mentoring scenarios set in different circumstances, followed by some suggestions for the way a mentor might act in each case. We hope that you will find them helpful.

Good luck.

9

Mentoring Scenarios

SCENARIO 1

A has worked for the same organisation since leaving school ten years ago with three GCSEs, including maths and English, but has undertaken no further academic studies since schooldays. A has done well in his department and has had several promotions. However, his knowledge of other parts of the organisation, and of any other part of the commercial/industrial sector, is very limited.

The boss considers that A is vital to the department as he has so much knowledge and experience and all the other staff are relatively new. A knows the systems and procedures inside out.

The organisation has decided to introduce a mentoring system to help staff to progress within the company and as an aid to retaining their best staff. A has asked to join the scheme as he feels that he is getting into a rut.

If you were the mentor assigned to A, how would you plan your approach to the task and how would you prepare for your initial meeting with him?

SCENARIO 2

B has been employed within an organisation as a trainee on a three-year training contract. Part of the contract involves studying for a qualification through day release at a nearby college. There is no guarantee of employment at the end of training, but it is expected that, provided that progress is maintained in their studies and practical work, the majority of trainees will move into substantive posts upon qualification.

Recently, the organisation has introduced a mentoring scheme for all trainees. B is already in the second year of training, having completed the first year successfully. She has passed all her examinations and has received good reports on her practical work. However, Year 2 is proving a little more difficult. Interim test results from the college are not good and the workplace reports are not as good as in Year 1.

Because of the timing of the introduction of the mentoring scheme, the person appointed as mentor for B has to take up the role midway through Year 2.

Unbeknown to her managers, college staff and the mentor, B has been experiencing personal problems. These are concerned with financial difficulties and the break-up of a relationship.

If you were the mentor assigned to B, how would you deal with the situation and how would you react to the poor performance at college and to the personal problems if and when you discover the facts?

SCENARIO 3

C is a senior manager within an organisation which he joined initially in a middle management post. The first four years have been very successful and quite satisfying, with two promotions, the second being into senior management. However, C now feels he has been sidelined into a job which, although interesting, is away from the mainstream, and he is rapidly losing out in relation to future promotion prospects. Consequently, he has asked to be included in the organisation's mentoring scheme and a mentor has been allocated to him.

C's mentor comes from another department and, prior to taking up the mentoring role, did not know C. Initial meetings have taken place, but C does not feel confident he will benefit from the relationship or that his position in the organisation will be enhanced. The mentor has become aware of this, but feels strongly that his own personal reputation within the organisation will be at stake if he fails to achieve any success as a mentor.

If you were the mentor, how would you tackle the situation in order to gain the confidence of the mentee?

SCENARIO 4

D is a clerical officer within an organisation. She has no strong ambitions other than to earn enough money to support herself and to enjoy her particular outside interests. Gaining more responsibility at work and studying for a relevant qualification, in themselves, do not appeal.

The organisation feels very strongly that each employee should have a mentor to help them to develop their potential, however limited that may be. D feels that, for her, this is not necessary. Also, she has suspicions that the mentor is yet another link in the chain of control. Although she has met with the mentor on a number of occasions, she only goes through the motions because it is organisational policy and she doesn't want to be seen to be rocking the boat.

How does the mentor overcome this attitude and approach and convince D there is something to be gained by participating fully in the scheme?

SCENARIO 5

E is a high-flyer who is considered to be chief executive material. His current employer head-hunted him and is determined to hold on to this star acquisition. Consequently, it has been decided to allocate a mentor to E, and a very senior member of staff has been chosen for this role. This person has been with the organisation for many years, has been chief executive within a subsidiary company and now holds a board-level post with the group headquarters. Having taken on the role, the mentor is acutely aware of the need to ensure that E is developed according to his potential and, as the mentor, is determined to do everything in his power to help E to succeed and, more importantly, to remain within the organisation.

The first few months of mentoring have been fine, but now there is a growing suspicion that E is becoming restless and may have been approached by another organisation.

How should the mentor tackle this?

SCENARIO 6

F has always been a very conscientious and loyal individual who has performed well. Her mentor established a good relationship with her and things have gone smoothly in the past couple of years. However, recently, things have deteriorated.

F has come under increasing pressure, with several projects approaching a crucial point at the same time. Unfortunately, this has resulted in F cancelling several planned meetings with her mentor. The mentor has not been particularly bothered about this as the relationship has been very low-key for some time; they have grown so used to each other that they have begun to take things for granted. Eventually, when they do manage to meet, it is evident that the mentor has misread the situation and that F is in a state of near panic and needs help and guidance far beyond that which the mentor considers to be his mentoring role.

What should the mentor do about this situation and what lessons can be learned from it?

SCENARIO 7

G has had a mentor for several years during which he has progressed from being a young trainee to a fully qualified person. Having had the same mentor from the very beginning has been a distinct advantage. The relationship has worked very well and both parties have benefited from the experience – in fact the two have also become good friends. G is now seeking to develop his career and is considering options across a much wider spectrum, including branching out into another discipline or working at higher levels – possibly at the group headquarters or the organisation's head office in London. The mentor has been an excellent support whilst G was training and in the immediate subsequent years, but it has become apparent that his knowledge, sphere of influence and contacts outside the immediate location are very limited. In addition, G has progressed more rapidly than the mentor and now they are of almost equal seniority.

Both mentor and mentee wish to continue their mentoring relationship as it has been so successful, but the mentoring scheme co-ordinator foresees the difficulties that lie ahead and the consequent limitations on G's future progress.

Both mentor and mentee are having difficulty in agreeing to end the relationship. How could this have been avoided? And what can now be done to ensure that the foreseen difficulties are overcome?

SCENARIO 8

H has worked in a production department of an engineering company for a number of years and, during that time, has become proficient in all the manufacturing processes performed in the department. Recently, the company has introduced a scheme of 'induction mentoring' for all new employees. This will entail the induction mentor in each department welcoming each new employee on their first day and introducing them to their duties, colleagues and the wider department. They will also be responsible for the initial on-the-job training the new employee will receive. This approach will complement the general induction process undertaken by the Human Resources department on the first day of employment. In recognition of H's diverse skills and extensive knowledge of the production processes, the boss has asked him to be the induction mentor for the department.

How should H prepare for this new role? What skills and qualities do you think he will need to undertake it successfully?

SCENARIO 9

J is a first-class honours graduate who, on graduating, worked within a commercial organisation. Just over a year ago, she decided on a career change and obtained a lecturing post at a college of further education. This seemed to be an attractive prospect as, in addition to teaching vocational courses in her own subject, there would be the possibility of undertaking postgraduate research, possibly leading to a doctorate.

However, towards the end of the first academic year, things have not gone well. Much more work than expected is involved in preparing lecture material and in setting and marking course assignments, all of which have to 'verified' on behalf of the body that awards the qualification. Much of this work is having to be done at home, out of college hours. Also, so far, there has been little time to consider any form of research. Another factor causing J some concern is that, although the majority of students are very receptive and keen to learn, a small faction seems to be uninterested, arriving late and interrupting the flow of the lessons.

J has tried to raise her difficulties with her immediate supervisor but, although this person is supportive, he is also very busy with his own duties and hasn't a lot of time to deal with J's problems. J has now heard that the college is to introduce a mentoring scheme for the benefit of staff and has expressed an interest in being allocated a mentor.

How could a mentor help in these circumstances, and what preparation should they undertake in order to begin to establish a good relationship with their mentee?

SCENARIO 10

K is a professional pianist who has recently joined a mentoring scheme set up by the local education authority to support gifted schoolchildren. Following the required vetting procedures, K is to be mentor to an 8-year-old who is learning to play the piano. The child concerned is very keen, has piano lessons at school and also practises there, because there is no piano at home.

From initial meetings with the mentee, K is confident that, given the necessary encouragement and support, she could progress to a high level of professional musicianship. The big problem, however, is the lack of facilities in the child's home. The parents are not very well off and the family does not have any musical background or any apparent interest in music. However, the head of the school has told K the parents always show a keen interest in their child's welfare and academic progress and have expressed a willingness to do everything they can to foster her musical development.

What options does the mentor have in trying to help her mentee and what steps might she take to try to ensure that the mentee is given whatever support she needs in order to achieve her musical potential?

POSSIBLE APPROACHES TO THE MENTORING SCENARIOS

Scenario 1

In this case it is essential that the mentor is able to convince the mentee (A) of the independence of their mentoring role and that they have his best interests at heart. At the same time it is important that the mentee's line manager does not feel threatened by what they might consider to be 'interference' by a third party. The mentor should plan a strategy which allows the mentee to think about his long-term future: what he would like to do, what additional knowledge and experience he needs to acquire, how he can best use his current job to achieve these aims. At the same time it would be useful to establish a relationship with the mentee's boss to let them know how the mentor's role will fit in with the best interests of the organisation and the employee. The mentor needs to gain the confidence of the line manager and to assure them that, by helping the mentee through his development process, the best interests of the organisation in general will be best served. The line manager should also be made aware of the confidential nature of the mentoring relationship.

The initial meeting with the mentee should be one of 'setting the scene', making sure agreement is reached upon the boundaries of the relationship, the objectives and the means and frequency of communication. The mentee will need to be reassured that he is highly valued by the organisation and that the mentoring process will build on his current strengths.

SCENARIO 2

The first thing you would need to do in the case of B, is to ensure that you have all the details of the mentee's record to date, her work and academic background.

An early meeting with the mentee should be held to establish the relationship and, without being too intrusive, perhaps get some clues as to the problems being experienced in Year 2. It is essential at this early stage in the relationship to build up confidence of the mentee. Look at the positive aspects of the first year: the success in the examinations and the good reports in the workplace. Encourage the mentee to talk to you about how she feels she is progressing to date. Above all, don't be critical at this early stage about her poor results and reports in Year 2. By building up her confidence and establishing a rapport with her, she should soon feel able to discuss her problems with you. However if you push the mentee too hard at the start she may well feel you are criticising her and will be reluctant to discuss any problems openly.

If you suspect that personal problems are causing the present difficulties, encourage the mentee to talk about her life outside the workplace, but don't be too direct. Leave it to her to volunteer information if and when she is ready to do so. If you do discover the facts about her financial and relationship difficulties be sympathetic. Try to suggest solutions to the college and workplace issues, but don't try to solve her personal problems. That is not the role of the mentor and you should ensure that both you and the mentee understand this and where the boundaries are within your mentoring relationship.

SCENARIO 3

The initial meetings with the mentee (C) have obviously not given any indication of any tangible benefits to the mentee, who is probably feeling a bit down anyway. The fact that you as the mentor are from a different department probably adds to the mentee's feelings that not much will be done for him. Therefore, in order to show that things can be improved and to start to build the confidence required, you need a 'success', no matter how small. You also need to show that you have done your homework and that you have the qualities and skills required to help the mentee. Whereas, in the normal course of events, the mentor's role is one of 'helping the mentee to help themselves', in this instance some more direct help would show the benefits of having you as a mentor. Try to find something the mentee feels unhappy about and use your networks and contacts to try to improve his situation. Remember, however, that you must be aware of the roles of others who come into contact with the mentee and don't try to do their jobs. Remember, also, that you must not under any circumstances instigate any actions without the consent of the mentee.

SCENARIO 4

With mentee C, you must first overcome the suspicion that you are part of the line management and are there simply to check up on the mentee's progress. Secondly, you will have to convince her that mentoring is all about helping her to achieve what she wants from the organisation and that this can be something quite basic such as enjoying what she does. Emphasise to her that it does not mean, necessarily, that she must be always striving for promotion or studying for further qualifications.

One way of achieving this is to ensure you meet with the mentee in an informal setting whenever possible. Try to use a conversational style and chat to her about the things she enjoys. Hopefully, in this way, you will begin to establish a rapport with her. You can then introduce work issues by posing questions such as:

- 'What do you like about coming to work?'
- 'What don't you like about coming to work?''
- 'Do you feel satisfied when you leave work at the end of the day that you have achieved anything and, if not, why do you think that is?'

In this way you will slowly build up a picture of what she wants from her employment and hopefully, in time, you will get her to think about what she needs to improve her working life.

SCENARIO 5

How the situation with E is tackled will depend upon the quality of the relationship that has been built up between you and the mentee and how frank a discussion you can have with each other. It will also depend upon how you have gained the suspicion that the mentee has been approached by another organisation. You may have heard it from a third party, or it may be simply a suspicion on your part from your conversations with the mentee. Remember, at this stage, it is a suspicion, not fact. Therefore, you should tread carefully and probably need to probe a little without divulging your suspicions directly and hope that you can get the mentee to reveal something. Perhaps even ask him if he has considered working for anyone else. Alternatively, perhaps you could invite him to sketch out for you his possible future career development, which might indicate whether or not he is looking elsewhere.

You do need to encourage your mentee to discuss things in a frank manner and to ensure that he has sufficient confidence in you to know that anything he tells you will be strictly confidential. Whether or not anything is revealed will depend entirely upon the mentee's perception of whether he will benefit from telling you. If he decides not to there is not much you can do. If he does decide to discuss the situation with you it probably means he feels the need to talk things over with someone he can trust. Don't try to talk him out of moving elsewhere solely because you think that would suit the needs of the organisation. The mentee would not thank you for that if it turns out to be the wrong decision. Be honest with him. Tell him that the organisation values him highly and would want him to stay, but be prepared to talk over the pros and cons of the situation with him. For the good of the organisation, the decision must be his and, as his mentor, you must respect that.

SCENARIO 6

In this situation it is imperative that the mentor stays calm and brings the situation into perspective. Start by getting the mentee (F) to list all of her problems and then decide which ones you can help with or give guidance on. Encourage her to tackle those where you can be of direct help. Usually, in such circumstances, some quick successes help to ease the pressure and make the mentee feel better. For the remaining problems, even if you are not able to help F directly, merely by bringing some order and calm to the situation and simply by being there and being someone for her to talk to will help.

For those areas where you feel unable to help directly you may still be able to offer some ideas the mentee hasn't thought of already. In addition, although some of the problems are outside your scope as a mentor, you may be able to use your network of contacts to put the mentee in touch with someone who can help them. Above all, don't panic. It is rarely the case that nothing can be done to improve a situation. Try to help the mentee to draw up a plan of action and, if necessary, convince her of the need to talk to her superiors about her difficulties. Most bosses would rather know about problems before they become insurmountable.

As regards lessons to be learned, this scenario illustrates the need for the mentor always to stay in touch with their mentees on a regular basis, even when things are going well. Small problems often turn into major ones if they are not recognised and action taken early. You should never take your mentee for granted. Draw up a strategy with them and ensure that both of you stick to it.

SCENARIO 7

It is important at the beginning of any mentoring relationship to agree the boundaries, the objectives and the exit strategy. This must be monitored closely and reviewed regularly. Had that been done in G's case it would have become clear at a much earlier stage that the relationship would have to end at some point and arrangements could have been made to ensure this was achieved without any undue hassle. Indeed, the current mentor could have assisted in helping to find a new mentor for G. The second point to bear in mind is the degree to which the personal friendship has developed. By all means become friendly with your mentee but always remember that you need to remain independent and don't become too familiar, otherwise you may start to confuse the issues.

The mentoring scheme co-ordinator will now need to discuss the situation with both parties and try to reach a compromise. There is no reason why the two should not remain good friends, but this should not be confused with the mentoring role. The mentor should be able to use their knowledge of the mentee and his requirements and styles to assist in finding a suitable mentor for the future.

SCENARIO 8

As initial preparation, H should familiarise himself with the general induction carried out by the Human Resources department. This will be important so as to ensure that there is no conflict between the information and advice given to new employees by them and that given by H within the production department. Then, H will need to prepare a departmental induction programme that will give a comprehensive and consistent introduction to all new employees of the department. Ideally, it would be useful to produce a brief guide for each new employee, giving details of all the 'rules' and 'customs' of the department in which they will be working. An introduction to colleagues should also be part of the programme. As H will also be expected to help with any problems that new employees may encounter in their initial period of employment, he should make the necessary arrangements to be available.

The next stage in the process should be the initial on-the-job training. A planned approach to this should be prepared and a process drawn up to be followed in the initial training period of each new employee. Regular spot checks should be built in to enable H to ensure that everything is satisfactory and the required competences are being achieved so that, after this initial training, any further training can be undertaken by the person responsible for training within the department. H will need to have good planning skills, be able to communicate easily, be prepared to listen and, when necessary, to motivate individuals to carry out the tasks allocated to them.

SCENARIO 9

Because the mentoring scheme is a new venture within the college it will be particularly important for the mentor to act sensitively both in the interests of J and in contributing to the development and, hence, the reputation of the scheme. In this case the mentor should be able to offer J an independent and confidential contact with whom to talk through her problems and difficulties. The mentor might also be able to use their own network of contacts within the college to enlist support for J.

However, before meeting with the mentee, the mentor should find out as much as they can about her background, current work and future prospects. This will include familiarising themselves on the courses J is teaching and the requirements of the body that awards the qualifications for which the students are preparing. As part of this investigative process the mentor should also speak informally with J's current supervisor. At a later stage, and with J's consent, and using this initial contact as a baseline, the mentor might be able to broker a meeting between the mentee and her boss in order to discuss the difficulties being experienced.

The problems facing J essentially are of time and work management and dealing with certain factions of students. Therefore, in meetings with J, the mentor should be supportive and helpful, but they should also be realistic and encourage J to try to find for herself a range of solutions that might be possible. The mentor could then review these with J and encourage her to reach appropriate solutions by reviewing the pros and cons of each. As far as further training is concerned, time and work management skills could be advocated as also could the possibility of J undertaking a formal teacher training course as this would include guidance on the matters currently causing difficulty.

SCENARIO 10

K needs to build up a relationship with the child's parents and the music teacher as well as with the child if the objective of helping her to achieve maximum potential is to be realised. It is important that the child, as the mentee, understands how the mentor can help him and what his role is. He will also need to have clearly defined boundaries so that he does not confuse the role of the mentor with that of the teacher. The mentor should be in a position to use his contacts within the music profession to help the mentee to make progress in areas outside the teacher's remit or where she does not have time to become involved. The mentor should also be able to give advice on the pace of development of the mentee's musical skill.

By building up a relationship with the parents the mentor can become aware of the facilities and resources available to the mentee at home and can suggest possible sources of help if necessary. For example, K will probably be aware of any grants, bursaries or support schemes that are available and whether they are appropriate for the mentee. He might have access to pianos or practice facilities that could be available to the mentee out of school hours. Although the mentor should not attempt to take on the teaching role, it is important she keeps in close contact with the teacher. The mentor should also bear in mind that any tutorial advice should be given through the teacher and not directly with the pupil.

Index